Rise Up
and
Do It

*Empowering Habits
That Make You
Stand Out*

Atinuke Olanrewaju

Inside Information

----------------CR----------------

There are hundreds of books on success habits on Amazon and everywhere, so what makes this one unique?

Whether you are just starting out in life or at any point in your life pursuit, 'Rise Up and Do It 'would show you how your habits affect your result, and reveals to you those habits that will get you win again and again.

This is a must read for anyone who wants to build a formidable character that weathers the storms in Business, Career, Health, Relationship and Personal life.

Make a decision to Rise Up to life challenges and do whatever it takes as you journey through life to your destination of achievement and success.

'Rise Up and Do It' will not only show those required success habits but also walks you through on how to identify, develop and improve on them.

In this book are inspirational stories of those who have taken on board some of the things shared within it which will be great motivation to you, the reader.

Dedication and Acknowledgement

--------------------CR--------------------

Dedication

To all out there, including you reading this book who will not stop seeking information on self-improvement until they achieve the optimum in life.

Acknowledgements

This book is a milestone achievement in view of the long journey ahead in the next phase of my life. I am forever grateful to God Almighty for making this possible. My gratitude goes to you, the reader for having faith in me by getting this book.

I couldn't have written this book without the support and encouragement of my husband, *Samuel* (*My number one fan and critic*) who at various stages of writing e the push and nudge I needed. Thank you for your love and unwavering belief in me. My world is a restful place because you are in it.

Writing my wall of appreciation would not be complete without mentioning my children; *Mololuwa, Pelumi and Bolurin.* You guys rock and make me proud every time. Thanks a million for your support and the peace of mind you have always given me. The universe will respond to you all as you have done to me.

Chapters Ahead

------------CR------------

'Rise Up and Do It' is a self-help book that unveils the role habits play in achieving set goals in any pursuit in life. Habits can be learned and unlearned. They are muscles, once you learn how to flex them, you'll be able to use them meet life's challenges and fulfil your goals.

In 'Rise Up and Do It', Atinuke leads you through a series of discussions, stories, recommendations, and exercises designed to help you create a different experience in your lives. She shares invaluable insights you can use to gain confidence to do what you've always wanted and overcome obstacles that hamper you from achieving our potential.

Topics in this book include;

- *Don't try - DO*

- *Excuses are self-defeating*

- *Believe you are a doer and achiever and you'll become one*

- *Build resilience by reinforcing what you do rather than what you accomplish*

- *Become open to learning from your own experience and from those around you.*

The human brain is complex and is always working with your ego to sabotage your best intentions. But once you are aware of this, you can create habits that will better your life.

This book is organised into 11 chapters with the 1st chapter introducing you to how people wish to be successful without understanding what it really means to be a success.

In chapter 2, there is a brief overview of what habit is, how to understand its framework, how habits are formed, its relationship with your character and its impact on the results you'll achieve in life.
Additionally the myth of the popular 21 days habit formation is exposed. The 3Rs of habit formation is discussed in full to gain a holistic understanding of how behaviours evolve.
*This book groups habits into the **5** important areas of life; the success in all 5 areas makes you whole,*

giving you a proud feeling of accomplishment. The said areas are;

1 Health   **2 Relationship**

3. Career/ Business   **4.Finances**

5 .Personal/ Self Development

In Chapter 3, you will be exposed to the 6 healthy living habits that are needed to support the framework of success. No one wants to spend the first half of his life becoming wealthy and successful and later have to spend all the wealth accumulated addressing health issues. Healthy habits are the foundational habits on which all other habits are built. If health is neglected, when a crash comes in other areas, there will be no foundation to hold you up. So it is important to rearrange your priorities and put things in proper perspective.

Chapter 4 focuses on building great relationships and sustaining them. There are 2 particular habits that will deliver to you what money cannot buy i.e. a quality, enriched life. Relationships with people matter, especially relationships with those that will be there when we are dealt life blows and bad shots.

Chapter 5 explores 4 habits that are core to our career or business success. Although they may appear insignificant to getting to the top of the ladder of success, they are vital in the climbing and remaining at the top of the ladder.

Chapter 6 deals with the 3 finance habits necessary for anyone to attain financial freedom. Financial freedom does not necessarily equate to extreme wealth, rather, it means being financially successful, enough to meet all one's needs.

Chapter 7 connects the 4 groups of habits earlier explored in the book together. It is on personal or self-development. 5 habits are identified and delved into deeply.

Chapter 8-11 deals with information we need to know on how to effectively develop and improve in all areas of life. One is also made aware of the possible reasons for the failure of past efforts that one has made to develop and maintain good habits .

It is not enough to be equipped with all the habits explored, but more importantly, one must act on them. The last 4 chapters reveal how you can develop and/or improve on the discovered habits. It also shares inspirational stories of those that have done so before. These are the 'action chapters' which give life to those habits.

These chapters will teach you things you can do differently to achieve your long desired result.

Come along with me as we take the journey together!

About the Author

Atinuke is a Chartered Accountant, Consultant, Public speaker and Executive Coach. She is the founder of March2One Concept, a coaching and consulting organisation in the UK.

Atinuke loves supporting individuals and corporate organisations, either on a voluntary or professional basis to maximise potentials. She coordinates a UK-based young people's charity.

Atinuke's personal statement is 'to make a positive and lasting difference' to every individual and organisation she comes across in life. She is an ardent believer that everyone has a talent waiting to be discovered and utilised.

Rise Up and Do it! is Atinuke' s debut book, published to guide readers through the different habits that successful people have and encouraging readers to proactively adopt these habits.

If these habits are turned into actions, the sky would be the limit. There is a giant in you waiting to manifest!
I would be happy to hear from you after reading this book. Please send me an email at premierpublishers@gmail.com

RISE UP AND DO IT

Contents

1. Why ' Rise Up and Do It' ?

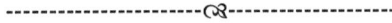

----------------------CR--------------------

You've made it! Your life's perfect and you're so successful at everything you do that it hurts. NO? I guess that's why you've picked this book.

> "Good habits are hard to form and easy to live with. Bad habits are easy to form and hard to live with. Pay attention. Be aware. If we don't consciously form the good ones, we will unconsciously form the bad ones. " *Mark Matteson*

For a long time, I've wondered how people who are unrelated or even live in different continents and are in different walks of life have so many similarities when I read about their lives. If you read biographies, you may identify with this.

Why do you think you have been successful in reaching some of your goals but not others? If you are not sure, then you are not alone in this confusion.

Have you not read, listened to or watched interviews of highly accomplished people and you find them lousy when it comes to describing how they succeeded? There is this intuitive answer – that you're born with certain talents – well, this is just a small piece of the puzzle. There are so many talented people who made no mark with their talents.

Decades of research has revealed that successful people reach their personal and professional goals not because of those seemingly intrinsic traits (talents, skill sets or gifts), but because of who they have become by the things they have done. This has empowered them to have whatever they set their minds at doing. If presented with another opportunity, completely different from what they have already accomplished, there is a very high propensity that success would be replicated again and again. Why is this so? 'Rise Up and Do It' offers an answer!

This got me curious to research those things that successful people have in common as said things must be a reason for their achievements in life.

This book is about those things they do and how they do them. It will give you a peep into the mind-set that drove them to push through until they achieved their goals.

'Rise Up and Do It' is about small things that are done daily or regularly which make a BIG difference in the life of the doer.

We all have habits; some good, others bad. The good ones benefit and empower us. They navigate us toward achieving or realising our worthy goals while the bad ones do nothing but steal our peace and fulfilment, and hinder our success.

A habit is a recurrent, often unconscious pattern of behaviour that is acquired through frequent repetition. About 40% of everything we do is done merely from habit. If you are reading this book, it is probably because you have formed a habit of reading.

Others who desperately need the information in this book may not get it, simply because they have not formed a habit of reading. They are the ones who claim to "hate reading". If you repeatedly say you hate a thing, you are sending messages to your subconscious which are then replayed back to you, hence, making whatever it is harder to do. Remember, you become what you think about (whether good or bad)!

Good habits can be developed and any bad habit can be broken through determination. Some experts said that a habit can be formed or broken in thirty days, so I invite you to give it a try - change your life by changing your habits. At first, it may be difficult, but diligence and patience will eventually lead to success. One of the reasons we don't develop the good habits we say we want is because we live in a culture of an instant gratification; we are driven by immediate results. We want everything now and don't realize that many of the good things we want and need are not attained just because we want them. Good habits come to those who are persistent and refuse to quit. Vince Lombardi said, "Winning is a habit; unfortunately, so is losing." He also said, "Once you learn to quit, it becomes a habit."

Make that decision right now that you can and will be a winner at forming any good habit you want to form and breaking any bad habit that you want to break. Never start a project with doubt and fear of failure. Begin reading this book with the simple belief that change is a possible. You can become a better person by developing better habits or changing the habits that derail you from your desired goals.

2 - The Meaning and Concept of Habit

----------------------CR----------------------

What is Habit?

A habit is a routine of behaviour that is repeated regularly and tends to occur unconsciously. It is an acquired behavioural pattern regularly followed until it has become almost involuntary.

The Anatomy of Habit

Habits are things we learn to do through repetition and eventually do either unconsciously or with very little effort. We are what we repeatedly do. Don't be deceived into thinking that you can't help what you do, because

> *'We first make our habits and then our habits make us'*
>
> *Anonymous*

the truth is that you can do or not do anything if you really want to.

When you concentrate on the good things you want and need to do, it helps you overcome the bad things that you do not want to do.

One of the ingredients of forming good habits and breaking bad ones is focusing on what you want to do and not on what you want to stop doing. For example, if you overeat and want to form balanced, healthy eating habits, don't think about food all the time! Don't read cookbooks that are filled with beautiful, mouth-watering desserts, but instead read a good book on nutrition that will educate you on how to make better choices. Start to get busy and do things that will keep your mind off food. If you want to form a habit of regular exercise, don't think and talk about how hard it is, but think about the results you will have if you are persistent. Yes, you will have to invest time that you may not think you have to spare, and yes, you will get very sore in the beginning.

Habit Forming

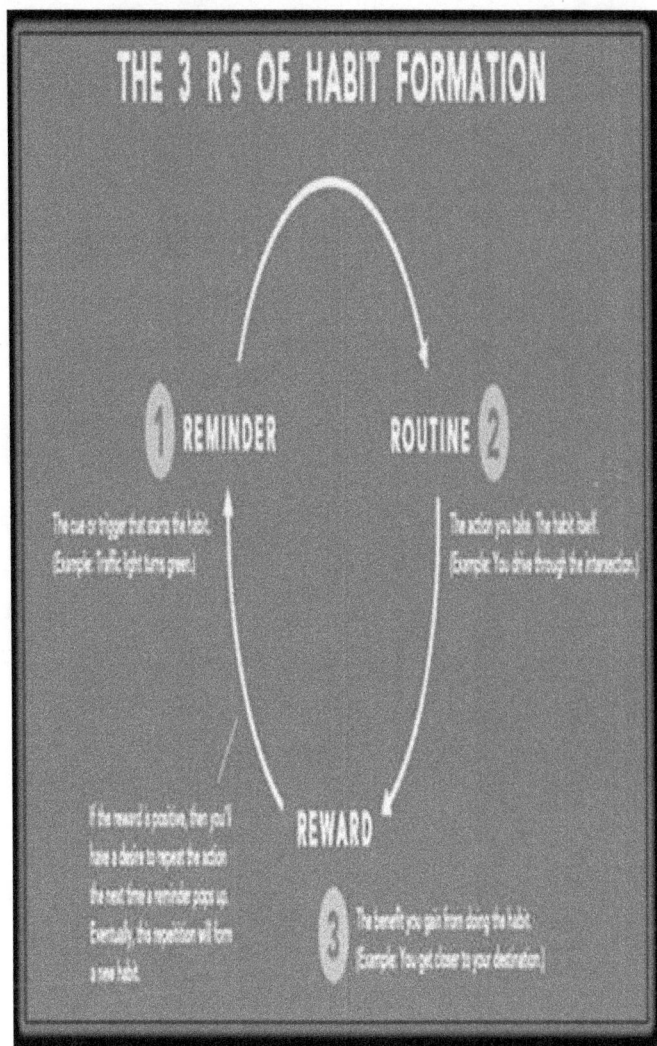

THE 3 R's OF HABIT FORMATION

① REMINDER
The cue or trigger that starts the habit.
(Example: Traffic light turns green.)

ROUTINE ②
The action you take. The habit itself.
(Example: You drive through the intersection.)

If the reward is positive, then you'll have a desire to repeat the action the next time a reminder pops up. Eventually, this repetition will form a new habit.

REWARD
③ The benefit you gain from doing the habit.
(Example: You get closer to your destination.)

The Reminder:

This can be an object, system or even a person. In forming a new habit, it is helpful if you can create a reminder process for yourself. It may be in setting an object of 'reminder' (like placing a small bottle of water in your car, office and other visible places in your home as a reminder to drink more water). It could be sounds, images, feelings and sensations.

The Routine

This is the act itself, in this sense, drinking water.

The Reward

The benefit derived from the act (habit), i.e. maintaining a healthy lifestyle.

Relationship between Habit and character

One of the outcomes of my research on habits and its relationship with our thoughts and character is illustrated in the diagram below, which I have named the ***Destiny Wheel.***

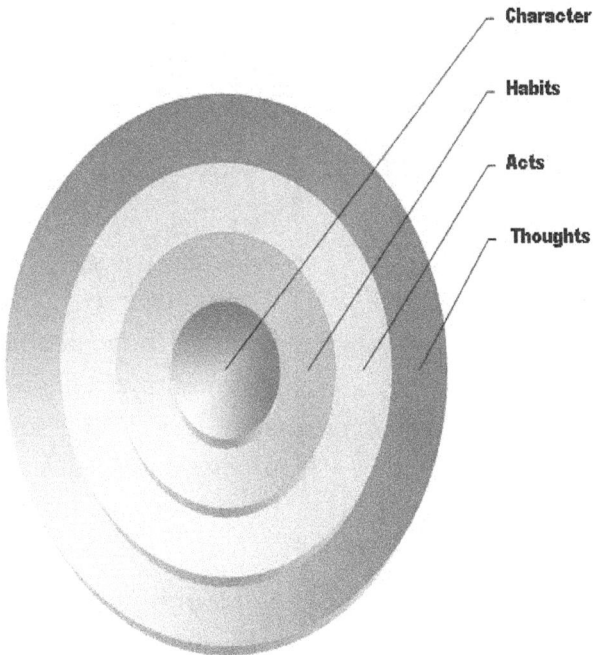

Character

Habits

Acts

Thoughts

From this diagram, it is clear that there is a distinct relationship between your thoughts and your character which describes who you are or who you become.

A combination of other factors may also influence who you become, but the foundation on which all the other factors are built lies in this **Destiny Will** diagram.

> *"Your beliefs become your thoughts,*
> *Your thoughts become your words,*
> *Your words become your actions,*
> *Your actions become your habits,*
> *Your habits become your values,*
> *Your values become your destiny."*
>
> — Mahatma Gandhi

I am going to be dwelling on the evidence we see which forms character and which clearly identifies and describes one; be it in one's personal, professional, business or spiritual life.

Habit as a Foundation

Like any building, the structure - the type of building you plan to construct, will influence the foundation you make. The life of an outstanding person is like a tower or a skyscraper; its foundation is higher than the height of other buildings because of the weight it has to carry. The things not visible to the eye are more important than the things that are. Using a building as a classical example, the foundation of the building, though unseen, is the backbone of the building. Without it there would be no edifice showing the architectural design we all see and admire.

The higher the building, the deeper and stronger the foundation must be, to be able to carry its weight, especially in the stormy times.

Habit and People

I am of the opinion that if you know and can easily recognise these habits, you would be able to make informed decision on the people you keep as close associates.

It is a well-known fact that your closest associates reflect the quality of your living *and even* the financial success you attain. In fact, it is said that *"you are the average of the closest five associates in your life"* i.e. their *habits, success, values, beliefs and even failures.*

Take a moment and check your five closest associates now!

Am I suggesting you change all your close friends and associates who do not have this foundational structure in their lives? *Yes and No.*

Yes, if you intend to achieve your goals or dreams in life and your current close associates do not have the values and beliefs that support you in this and **No,** if the values and belief systems of your current close associates support your life goals and aspirations.

Our values and beliefs systems drive our thoughts, eventually forming the habits that translate to the character we build and display.

Everyone cannot be outstanding because it takes extra effort to stand out. By default, there is a minimum standard that is attainable by everyone, but for you to go above that minimum and reach for the optimum, you must put in extra efforts.

In the Wheel of Destiny *"HABIT"* is number 3 in the hierarchy. Why number 3? This is the level at which you can see tangible evidence without looking too far;

they are visible in your speaking, (re)actions, responses and relationships with people on a daily basis. They are easily visible, but at the same time invisible if that is not what you are looking for.

It's amazing how habits can both attract and put away success.

It is needless to say that habits are results of daily acts; hence, they are easy to read, and with repetition over the years, will become part of you. When people describe you, they do so based on the habits you exhibit on a daily basis in your dealing with them.

The daily habits of outstanding people in all walks of life tend to go unnoticed by those who have them. *Why?* Because the habits are done unconsciously as they have become an integral part of the doers. *How?* They were originally thoughts that persisted for a long time until they became actions that have been repeated for so long, they have now formed parts of such people.

To achieve any outstanding goal in any area of life, you must understand the **BE-DO-HAVE** philosophy. *For you to achieve whatever you want to achieve you must first **BE** the person (character) of that goal then **DO** the* *things needed to achieve the goal, having the values and beliefs that support the goal in order for you to **HAVE** or achieve the goal.*

This goal could be in any area of life; *Career, Family, Health, Relationship, Finances, Spiritual, and Business,* etc.

This is the philosophy behind the success of every Olympian and prosperous person.

I am sure you're now curious to find out those regular habits that have become the common denominator for all achievers.

Generally, these habits are seen as what successful people do on a daily basis. They are the foundations that achievers have built on.

Those people with the "extra factor" have many comparable habits. Some are extreme; *ice cold showers, obsessive time keeping and daily chanting.* Others are more conventional; *daily prayer, maintaining regular eating habits, a catch-up telephone call to a parent or loved one.*

I set to group these habits into the **4** (plus 1) important areas of your life. Success in all 4 areas gives you a rounded feeling of accomplishment. Consequently, it is worth paying attention to all these areas as they are of equal importance and have equal impact on the accomplishment formula of life. It is not a wise decision to pay attention to a select few and neglect the others, as all these habits are interrelated.

These are the **4** main areas I will be focusing on *plus* the area that is common to all four;

   I.   Health
   II.   Relationship
  III.   Career/Business
  IV.   Finances
         PLUS
   V.   Self or Personal Development

The attention you pay to all these areas will reflect on the success achieved in the areas; however, it is necessary to note the impact they have on each other. For instance if you concentrate on your financial success without paying adequate attention to your health; you may end up achieving that financial success and spending half of the finances to maintain your health. This could have been avoided, if only you paid equal attention to your health habits too.

For you to enjoy the full benefits of your goals, it is worthwhile to assess all areas of your life to be able to highlight the areas you need to develop.

From the many habits identified, here are five broad categories of grouping them for ease of reference. In addition to the 4 important areas, there are also general success habits which are important for anyone that wants to live a successful or accomplished life.

Let us look at the following;

How do you butter your toast? How do you pack your case before going on holiday? How do you relax at the weekend? How do you deal with stressful situations? How do you respond to unruly road users? Your answer to each of these questions tells you something about your patterns of behaviour.

Some of your habits might be really useful, enjoyable and give you a great outcome. For instance, working out at the gym after a day of hard work, laying all of your holiday documentation out and checking it 100 times before you leave to go on holiday, having a quiet coffee on a Friday afternoon in your favourite coffee shop. Some habits may be less useful, maybe even destructive, such as aggressive driving or going to the pub every Thursday night and drinking 10 pints.

However, when habits kick in, you are usually not aware and so are not considering whether they are right or wrong. Your subconscious mind takes over and plays out a well-rehearsed set of actions that have been accumulated over the years. Do you sometimes recognise patterns of behaviour that are starting to have a negative effect on you and/or people around you? For example, eating when you are feeling down, snapping at a colleague who always (in your mind) makes stupid comments in team meetings, flopping down on the sofa in the evening rather than exercising.

If you have, then perhaps you are looking for a way to break those patterns of behaviour and create new habits - ones that will give you positive outcomes: that help you get fitter, lose weight, build better relationships at work, spend more time with your children, get ahead at work and so on. Developing new habits is remarkably simple to do (believe it or not!)

21 Days Habit Formation Myth

Is this line familiar? I am making New Year's Resolutions to start or stop doing... (whatever it may be)? If so, you may have been assured - usually by well-meaning fans of your attempted transformation - that you only need to stick with your resolution for 21 days for it to become an ingrained habit. How true is this? You're about to discover if you continue reading (Another habit which some find very hard to adopt - starting and finishing a book).

The magic number '21' is recurring in many write ups and articles I have read about forming a new habit or making a change to an existing one. Most of us know little of the origin of this '21 day' claim.

Psychologists have made it clear to us that habits are formed through a process called 'context-dependent repetition'. Let's take a typical example, imagine that each time you get home in the evening, you eat a snack. When you first eat the snack upon getting home, a mental link is formed between the context (getting home) and your response to that context (eating a snack). Each time you subsequently snack in response to getting home, this link strengthens, to the point that getting home automatically prompts you to eat a snack, without giving it much thought; a habit has formed.

Habits are mentally efficient: the automation of frequent behaviours allows us to conserve the mental resources that we would otherwise use to monitor and control these behaviours, and deploy them on more difficult tasks. Habits are likely to persist over time; because they are automatic and so do not rely on conscious thought, memory or willpower. This is why there is a growing interest, both within and outside of psychology, in the role of 'habits' in sustaining our good behaviours.

So where does the magic '21 day' figure come from?

It was tracked down to the source in the preface to a book written by *Dr Maxwell Maltz* in 1960 'PSYCHO-CYBERNETICS'. He was a plastic surgeon turned psychologist, who wrote:

'It usually requires a minimum of about 21 days to effect any perceptible change in a mental image. Following plastic surgery, it takes about 21 days for the average patient to get used to his new face. When an arm or leg is amputated, the "phantom limb" persists for about 21 days. People must live in a new house for about three weeks before it begins to "seem like home". These and many others commonly observed phenomena tend to show that it requires a minimum of about 21 days for an old mental image to dissolve and a new one to jell.'

How evidence from plastic surgery patients came to be generalised so broadly is ambiguous. 'Our self-image and habits tend to go together. Change one and you will automatically change the other. '

You may reason that if self-image takes 21 days to change, and changes in self-image lead to changes in habits, then habit formation must therefore take 21 days. However, although '21 days' may apply to adjustment to plastic surgery, it is unfounded as a basis for habit formation. So, if not 21 days, then, how long does it really take to form a habit?

In an excerpt from a university psychology research project on the study of habit formation (*Lally, van Jaarsveld, Potts, & Wardle, 2010*), the participants performed a self-chosen health-promoting behaviour (e.g. drinking a glass of water) in response to a once-daily cue (e.g. after breakfast), and gave daily self-reports of how automatic (i.e. habitual) the behaviour felt. Participants were under a tracking system for 84 days. Initial repetitions of the behaviour led to quite large increases in automaticity, but these increases then reduced in size; the more often the behaviour was repeated, until automaticit plateaued. Assuming that the point at which automaticity is highest is also the point when the habit had been formed, it took, on average, 66 days for the habit to form.

> *"H is for Habit, winners make a habit of doing the things losers don't want to do."*
> — *Lucas Remmerswaal*

Is it now obvious why you give up on a habit before it has fully crystallised?

Interestingly, there were quite large differences between individuals in how quickly automaticity reached its peak, although everyone repeated their chosen behaviour daily, for one person it took just 18 days, and another did not even get there in the 84 days.

A variation was also noted in how strong the habit became: for some people, habit strength peaked below the halfway point of the 42-point strength scale and for others; it peaked at the very top. It may be that some behaviours are more suited to habit formation – habit strength for simple behaviours (such as drinking a glass of water) peaked quicker than for more complex behaviours (e. g. doing 50 sit-ups) – or that people differ in how quickly they can form habits, and how strong those habits can become.

The bottom line is: stay strong. 21 days is a myth; habit formation typically takes longer than that. The best estimate is 66 days, but it's unwise to attempt to assign a number to this process. The duration of habit formation is likely to differ depending on who you are and what you are trying to do. As long as you continue doing any new behaviour consistently in a given situation, a habit will form. You will have to persevere beyond January 21st for the habit you have decided to form or change to materialise.

Changing Habits

All it requires is *time, patience and determination*.

If your aim is to change an existing habit, you have to replace the current behaviour or thought pattern (habit) with a new one; that can take up to 100 days. Think of your habit as a comfortable pair of shoes; you have worn them so many times that when you put them on you don't even know you are wearing them. They fit perfectly and enable you to go about your day as normal. You trust them because you know how they are going to look, what outfits they go with and the fact that they don't give you blisters.

You know that they are looking quite old now, and people are starting to comment on it but the alternative is going out there, trailing around hundreds of shops to try and find a replacement pair. You just know the process will be long and painful, and you still may not end up with such a good pair. So, you stick with what you know, despite the feedback people (perhaps including yourself) are giving you.

To change your habit, you need to consider what the benefits of that initial painful process of change will be.

What will this new habit give you? What will it enable you to do that you can't do now? How will it impact the important people in your life? Once you have given yourself a compelling reason to make the change, you then need to do 4 things:

> "It is health that is real wealth not pieces of gold and silver "
>
> *- Mahatma Gandhi*

i. *Become aware of the behaviour or thought that you want to change and specifically when it acts out.*

ii. *Every time you feel like doing that thing or thinking that thought, pause, take a breath and change your physiology or your environment.*

iii. *Identify what behaviour or thought you would like to have instead.*

iv. *Start doing it and keep doing it for at least 90 days.*

Then you will start to see the benefit.

You will have 'broken the new habit in', just like you do a new pair of shoes, and, if with consistent focus on your compelling reason, you will eventually be able to replace the old with the new and your new habit will crystallise to become part of your lifestyle.

In forming a new habit or replacing one, discipline is a key in addition to time and patience and determination.

Successful people do what they have to do to get the result they want.

This is called D. I. S. C. I. P. L. I. N. E.

3 - Health and Healthy Living Habits

--------------------∞--------------------

In this chapter, health habits are the first group to be considered because of their importance and significant impact on all other areas of life. It is often said; *"A healthy man is a wealthy man".* The success of other areas of your life can only be fully enjoyed when you have a healthy framework to support them. Hence, daily health habits are critical in the equation of any successful person be it, career, business or in your relationship with others.

The world is filled with unhealthy people, which is reflective on the number of visits to doctors and other medical practitioners. Billions of dollars are spent on medical consultations, medicines and treatments to help us feel better. The millions of hours spent on illnesses could have been avoided by cultivating healthy habits earlier in life.

Do not wait until you are sick before you choose to pay attention to your health and well-being. *An ounce of prevention is worth more than a pound of cure.* It has been observed that people who prioritise wealth over health sometimes spend the wealth gathered addressing medical issues in later years. It is wise to have cultivated healthy habits early on, allowing one to use their wealth for other worthy causes, other than medical treatments.

Habit 1: Early Riser

In most cases, those with the 'achievers trait' wake up early. The timing tends to vary, depending on the career of the individual. For people involved in the arts, music and entertainment, for example, rising at 10:00 am could be considered early, whereas for those in the military, 7:00 am is deemed as a long lie-in. However, it's customary for achievers to rise early, to plan or set the tone for the day. Rising early also depends on going to bed at the appropriate time so as to give the body the rest it needs.

Rise Up Indeed. Achievers do not stay in bed longer than necessary, except when on vacation, a time during which the intention is to rest. Their body systems have been so disciplined that once awake, they get out and get moving. The way you arise sets the tone of the day. Get up with all your body and mind. Do not linger around the bedroom if you may be tempted to hop back in to bed.

Habit 2: Healthy Eating

Getting the best quality nutrition into the body is important. Quality fuel feeds the body and brain. It also builds the immune system to resist foreign bodies that cause disease. Therefore, eating is a very important part of the day's schedule. You should enjoy food whilst being conscious of what you eat. Spend time planning and choosing the right foods. Choose what you eat based on its nutritional value and create meals you will enjoy. This impacts your energy level and thinking process.

Eat more fish, chicken, turkey and the likes, not fatty foods and red meat. If at all possible, eat organic hormone-free meat. The saying "we *are what we eat*" contains more truth than we may want to admit.

One of the cardinal guidelines on healthy eating is to do all things in moderation while having as much variety in your diet as possible.

> "Crash diets don't work. They don't work for losing weight, they don't work for making sales quota and they don't work for getting and keeping a job.
>
> The reason they don't work has nothing to do with what's on the list of things to be done (or consumed).
> No, the reason they don't work is that they don't change habits, and habits are where our lives and careers and bodies are made. "
> — *Seth Godin*

Fruits and vegetables are a must in our diet. Have you ever considered why the elephant is the strongest animal in the jungle and not the voracious lion? Check what it eats! It lives on grass, fruits, vegetables and plenty of water.

Habit 3: Hydrate

Experts recommend drinking half of our body weight of water every day. Drinking plenty of water improves your metabolism, supports weight loss and increases energy levels. The more water you drink, the more you will want to drink. If you are not drinking enough water, I urge you to start immediately.

If you cannot access pure clean water at home, buy a filter for it or buy bottled water. *To form the habit of drinking water is to keep it (water) with you at all times.* As you drink increasing amounts, you will notice a rise in energy levels, which will motivate you to sustain the habit.

Keep water as your main drink at home, in the office, car and any other place you are regularly. The fewer choices you have in your refrigerator or cabinets, the more inclined you will be towards water. Many people claim to dislike water; this is only because they are not accustomed to drinking it. Remember, your body will eventually crave what you give it regularly.

Water is the only thing that properly cleanses our bodies of dangerous toxins. Our bodies consist mainly of water. Because water is constantly evaporating, we must continually replace it.

Habit 4: Exercise is a way of life

Exercise is as important as eating and sleeping; its value is tremendous. There are multiple forms of exercise - I urge you to select one that suits you, one you can learn to enjoy, and turn it into a habit. Walk, ride a bicycle, swim, play an active sport, exercise with weights, or get an exercise video.

The choices are endless, so choose one and get started. Even if you feel that you cannot do a lot, doing something is better than doing nothing. Start small and build on it. Choose the most convenient time of the day for yourself so that it does not appear to you as a task.

Just make sure it's regular and a routine is formed with it – this is when it becomes a habit. Choose what your body and schedule of activities can take. Some people just make a habit of going to the gym 2 or 3 days a week while some prefer a daily 15 mins – 1 hour routine. Start small!

Habit 5: Rest and Sleep Well

Many complain of not having enough time to sleep the recommended eight hours a night. But the truth is that if you do not do so, you are probably running out of time faster than you think. You must plan rest and sleep to enjoy the wholeness of living.

Some people do not need as much sleep as others, but most of us need all we can get. If you are always tired, one of the questions to ask yourself is, "Am I getting enough sleep?"

Our lives can be shortened by not getting adequate rest. The mind doesn't function properly without sleep, and our immune systems are compromised and more apt to become unable to fight off disease. It is very interesting to me that God created us with the ability to shut everything down and sleep. Our bodies go into a state of renewal and repair during our sleep, and we are refreshed mentally, emotionally, and physically for the next day.

People who have trouble sleeping may need medical attention, but more often than not, the inability to sleep is stress related. It is also important to note that eating late at night affects your body because it is then burdened with the task of digesting the foods, when it should be resting, hence the reason you may wake up tired.

When you rest well, you sleep better. Rest does not necessarily mean, but can lead to, sleep. Form a habit of resting - a state of both mental and physical inactivity. Shut your system down from all the regular things you do and intentionally step into a state of relaxation.

Set a sleeping pattern that suits your work and lifestyle, making sure you get the recommended amount daily. There could be times when this is interrupted by unexpected circumstances, but ensure you get back to your pattern as soon as the interruption is over. Develop the healthy habit of regular sleep and rest, and you will enjoy the rest of your life much more.

Habit 6: Plan Short Breaks

Psychologists believe that people who use their holiday allowance in bursts rather than all in one go, are happier. You may have observed that you are happier when on holiday, and you tend to look forward to the holiday experience. Research confirms that people are happier when going on holiday than when coming back. You may want to give yourself the regular dose of happiness that short breaks have to offer. Imagine the satisfaction in experiencing this 3-4 times in a year!

It is said that those who take 'mini-breaks have more happy memories than those who holiday for an extended period of time. Plan this every year with a different purpose in mind. It could be just you, you and your spouse, you and your family or possibly you and your friends.

This means taking a holiday or a short break away from your work or business activities to avoid burning out. Holidays need not be expensive, especially if you cannot afford to travel. All it means is taking time out of your regular activities to engage in leisure activities that are relaxing and completely different from your normal activities. Spending a few days in a quiet or serene environment does a lot to your psychology and emotional wellness. Plan it each year and watch your productivity level shoot up.

However, if you can afford to change your environment and travel to places you are not familiar with, take a weekend visit to friends or family. This change of environment broadens your perspective of the world.

We all need a break from time to time, and opportunities for extended getaways might not come around as often as we'd like. This is where a short break can fit in perfectly, enabling you to go away for a few days and come back relaxed, refreshed, and ready to take on everyday life once again.

My Learning Points (Write down your learning points of this chapter)

....

....

....

Action Points

Habit(s) I want to continue (and when to do so ... Date)

....

....

....

Habits I want to change (and when to do so ... Date)

....

....

....

Congratulations! You made it to the end of this Chapter. The next one will be dealing with habits that are fundamental to helping you survive difficult times and challenging adversities.

4 - Relationship Habits

------------Cঙঽ------------

Healthy relationships are a vital component of wholeness and wellbeing. There is compelling evidence suggesting that strong relationships contribute to a long, healthy, and happy life. On the contrary, the health risks from being alone are comparable to the risks associated with cigarette smoking, blood pressure, and obesity.

Research shows that low social support is linked to a number of health consequences, such as:

- Depression which is the most common result of loneliness.

A research study also found a correlation between loneliness and immune system deregulation, meaning that a lack of social connections can increase your chances of sickness.

- Higher blood pressure. Decades of research supports the idea that a lack of relationships can cause multiple problems related to physical, emotional, and spiritual health. It is therefore undeniable that isolation is fatal.

Knowing how important relationships are to our wellbeing, one should make conscious and consistent efforts to develop and nurture them.

> 'Goodness is about character - integrity, honesty, kindness, generosity, moral courage, and the like. More than anything else, it is about how we treat other people.'
> —*Dennis Prager*

Habit 7: Appreciation, Kindness and Generosity

This is a 3 in 1 habit that engages your mind more than your physical body. It's a psychological one that shifts your way of thinking, eventually improving your self-esteem and boosting your confidence levels.

Appreciation

This habit develops your sense of gratitude. Appreciation makes you acknowledge other people and their acts. It is expressed by saying *"thank you"* for all acts of kindness received, regardless of who the person is. Gratitude can also be expressed by *paying compliments*. This habit helps you to look for the good in people, hence helping you to build a positive thinking attitude.

Appreciation also develops your *interest in others,* shifting the focus from yourself to those around you. Research shows that you spend more time with those who express an interest in you rather than those who are all about themselves.

The act of appreciation can help in curing pride as it is not self-focused as opposed to pride, which is. Proud people are selfish in their way of thinking which manifest in their actions. Proud people do not have healthy self-esteem, hence why they feel obliged to demean others.

My emphasis is on a continuous show of appreciation; some people are temporarily appreciative but unknowingly start looking for faults in others to make them feel good. Such people need to consciously force themselves to see others in a more positive light. This is about repeating an act until it becomes part of you.

Appreciation is a habit that needs to be cultivated right from thought level.

Kindness

There is nothing more valuable than an intentional act of kindness. Be intentional about kindness. Make it an integral part of you, with the mind-set of wanting to add value to the lives of people regardless of their race, sex, age or background.

Kindness is like a baton in a relay race, although it is leaving your hands, it is critical to your own success in the race. If the baton is dropped and not passed, the next runner may get to the finish line but will never win the race. The baton is vital in recording the win of the race, as is kindness in the winning of the race of life.

However, to be consistently kind to be consistently kind, you must value, believe and unconditionally love people. With this in mind, one should make relentless efforts in being kind to others.

Be intentional about it and the result will amaze you. Try it out on a daily basis, for the next 7 days, especially to those that you may not have the opportunity to see again, which makes the act unconditional.

Generosity

Generosity is showing a readiness to give more of something to a cause, person or project. A generous person is happy to give or share time, money, food, or whatever else with others. Generosity means freedom from meanness and smallness of mind or character. Greed (the opposite of generosity) has become a huge problem of humanity today. Greedy people are driven by selfish motives without due consideration to the effect of their decisions on others. Generosity is the answer to the problem of greed. The majority of people have a mindset of *"what's in it for me*?", but the influential people who have made a positive mark on this earth are not self-centred. Self-centeredness is a problem which makes a person unappreciative. Generosity is a habit that successful people have. Bill Gates, Warren Buffet, Oprah Winfrey, etc regularly give part of what they have to specific causes, people and even nations.

It was not a habit that they suddenly developed when they became successful. Look for needs in other people's lives that you can meet by giving part of the little or much that you have. The needs are always there, you may not see because you do not look out for them. The generous see the world differently. Let me highlight 9 ways they view things:

> *"Give what you have. To someone, it may be better than you dare to think."* —Henry Longfellow

1. They recognize that the resource pie is not finite.

Do not have a competitive mindset; thinking that your resources only grow when someone else's shrinks is a kind of thinking based on a faulty premise. It assumes that the size of the 'pie' is limited, and if someone else enjoys success, my opportunity shrinks. Frankly, this is an incorrect thinking pattern. The pie of resources is not finite. It continues to grow as society benefits from others' successes.

2. They believe that generosity leads to greater happiness.

Research has confirmed what generous people already know: giving increases the happiness, fulfilment, and purpose in the life of the giver. We were not created to be creatures of selfishness. Rather, we were designed to search for and discover happiness in loving and caring for others. Those who decide to look for fulfilment in the pursuit of happiness quickly discover it.

3. They acknowledge that success happens in helping others succeed.

The easiest path to finding success in your life is to help someone else find theirs. After all, our contribution to this world has to be measured by something more significant than the size of our savings account. Your life will find its greatest significance in how you choose to live it - and how you help others to live theirs.

4. They realise that changing even one life is worthwhile.

Generous people are aware that the world's problems cannot be solved by one person. To them, changing even one life within their sphere of influence is enough reward. This is a worthy cause that ought to be sought by all.

5. They trust others.

Generosity always requires trust. To be able to invest personal resources into another person, we must believe, that they will use them wisely. Generous people are optimistic and therefore happy people because they choose to live in a world where belief in others is liberally employed.

6. They dream big dreams for their money.

Your money is only as valuable as what you choose to spend it on. Generous people use their surplus to bring big dreams into reality. Your financial resources can be used to improve the quality of life for others. They can be used to make our communities safer, greener, and more responsible. Indeed, generous people dream big dreams for their money, as should we.

7. They have more resources to give than money.

We have so much more to offer this world than just financial resources: time, talents, experiences, and lessons learned. The generous think beyond their money; they also invest their lives into helping others. Often times, this gesture can be more difficult than signing a cheque, but usually, it is more desperately needed.

8. They plan to leave a legacy behind:

Generous people fully embrace the reality that life is short and we only get one shot at it. Those who fully embrace this reality learn to live life to the fullest. They recognize that we have but a short time to leave our print in the sand of time and they cheerfully give their resources to accomplish this.

9. They are content to live with less.

By definition, true generosity requires a level of contentment. It recognizes the reality that giving to others constitutes to less for oneself. However, the joy of seeing others happy brings great contentment. Generosity thus becomes the fuel for greater contentment.

Our world is desperately seeking cheerful and generous givers. We need them to improve the society for unborn generations. They inspire us, push us forward. We all need to get into the circle of the generous !

Habit 8: Family and Friends

Make Weekend Plans Ahead

After all the life drama in your business or career, you come to the set of people that are the supporting framework of your life. When you have made all the money (possibly!) and satisfied yourself with achieving your life ambitions, you then want to relax and enjoy fulfilment with your loved ones. Suddenly you realise that they are long gone because you have not nurtured those relationships.

Relationships need to be nurtured. Family relationships are no exception to this rule; they should not be ignored but interestingly, they are the ones we easily take for granted. Make that phone call, make the plan for visits, and create moments that would be good memories for the children and your spouse. Why not take a moment now, list the key relationships in your personal life and assess the quality of the bond or association. Taking stock will help you make decisions on the need to cultivate or improve the habit of developing relationships.

Successful people plan their weekends and time off work ahead. This enables them to spend quality time with people that are important to them, hence, building healthy relationships alongside building success in their careers and businesses. When you are pleased with the state of your relationships, it positively impacts your work life.

You cannot have rounded success if your relationships with family and friends are not healthy. People tend to spend more time on other areas at the expense of the key people in their lives. However, longer lasting success is sustainable and enjoyed when you have relationships; both formal and informal.

Make plans ahead to build these relationships by making the best of your weekends and free time.

Let me share with you the story of a man who, knowing that his job took him away from home most weekends, made sure that four of the five weekdays, he would pick his children up from school and spend the evenings with them. It got to a point where children saw their dad's behaviour as absurd, especially in comparison to the relationship between their friends and their dads. It was only when they grew up and were struggling to spend that much time with their own children that they realised how great an effort their Dad put in.

The same dad, now a grandfather, knowing how valuable relationships are, has formed a new habit of spending 3 hours every Saturday morning with his 2 grandsons. A *bond* is created in these regular 3 hour slots with Grandpa. Can money buy this? Of course not! This bond is as a result of the old man valuing family relationships and creating time for them in his lifestyle.

You can do same; plan walks, tea parties, cinema trips and birthday outings. Plan telephone calls to the people you cannot see regularly. Keep in touch with your spouses, parents, siblings and children during the day. This passes a message that they are on your mind.

Make your weekends count! Use them to nurture all the relationships that support you whilst you are out chasing your careers and businesses. You only have one life to live - make it count for you and your loved ones.

Choose to develop or improve this habit today!

My Learning Points (Write down your learning points of this chapter)

....

....

....

Action Points

Habit(s) I want to continue (and when to do so ... Date)

....

....

....

Habits I want to change (and when to do so ... Date)

....

....

....

How well do you rate in habits that develop/improve the key relationships in your life. Is there one or more habit you need to START, STOP, do MORE or LESS. *Make an action plan now!*

Rise Up and Do It"!

5 - Career / Business Habits

-------------------CR------------------------

Habit 9: To Do List

Because achievers make plan for each day of the week, these plans are broken down and written on paper. It's thinking on paper. This frees your brain for other things. Drawing up a to- do-list saves you a lot of brain racking every time you're faced with the question of what to do at any point in time. It takes off the stress of wanting to remember everything you need to do. Because its your guide for what needs to be done for the day or week.

The list can be anything ranging from business to relationship (i. e. Making a telephone call to parent or friend, making certain business calls, picking up gifts for loved etc.). The content is inexhaustible and varied. Anything can go on the list.

Daily *To-do List* is a must for achievers as **they** know that is a way to tackle problems and get more things done.

1. *Think of everything you need to do.* State it clearly, and use proper English. Instead of writing "grocery store," write, "Go to the grocery store to buy some more semi skimmed milk".

2. *Use good handwriting.* If you can't read it, what's the point?

3. *Make it noticeable.* Write in bright colours or put it in a noticeable place, because seeing it encourages doing it!

4. *Put a date or day on it.* It helps a lot if you know when to do it, so you can feel ahead of your schedule.

5. *Organize the list to get it done quickly.* If it's a Christmas list, group items by store or

shopping centre. Then organize it to minimize travel distance between stops. You can save hours by planning properly.

6. *Prioritize the most important things first.* If it's a repair list (around the house), put the most important problems first. If it's a big list, break it into manageable or incremental one-weekend or one-day projects.

Habit 10: Keeping Journal

Achievers capture every thought of the moment by keeping a journal. Keeping a notepad and a pen or pencil handy is an essential habit. Jonathan Raggett, a leading hotelier with a global responsibility for a range of hotels, has brilliant memory, but he carries a small pocket sized Moleski notebook in which he constantly records thoughts and ideas for improvements. It's not that he doesn't trust his memory or that he doesn't use electronic devices. His notes are a firm basis for his actions.

A further search into the lives of successful people revealed that they kept detailed journals of their lives. Those journals served two purposes: a permanent record for posterity, and cathartic release for the people writing them. Even if you don't think you need either, keeping a journal has great benefits which you can enjoy immediately. Here's why you might want to sit down regularly to jot down your thoughts

I. Regular Writing has Mental Health Benefits

Writing can do wonders for your health. Beyond keeping your creative juices flowing—regular writing can give you a safe, cathartic release valve for the stresses of your daily life. For example, keeping an awesomeness journal can do wonders for your self-esteem. Not only does regular writing make you feel good, it helps you re-live the events you experienced in a safe environment where you can process them without fear or stress.

II. *Keeping a Journal Helps Harness Your Creativity*

The creative benefits of keeping a journal are numerous. For example, regular writing can help you to learn a process and communicate complex ideas effectively. It can also help you to memorize important information and brainstorm new ideas. In other words, writing about your experiences not only helps you process them, but it also helps you see opportunities that may not have been apparent at first glance.

There are different mediums; paper form (in journal notebook, diary, other notebook, etc.) and electronic form. Choose a preferred one and start writing down those thoughts as they come to you. Capture your thoughts on paper or electronic medium, don't let them slip away.

Habit 11: Raising The Bar

The habit of raising the bar is the one that makes you improve on any goal/project's current level of progress. It cures the disease of mediocrity. It also solves the problem of stagnancy in your pursuit.

Continuously looking for ways to improve in any and every area of life will give you that competitive edge in your business or career or even in your spiritual life.

Achievers have this habit which makes them never settle for a level when a higher level can be achieved. This habit will impact positively in any area of your life that you apply it to.

The emphasis here is raising the bar or standard to make positive impact not to become a perfectionist. Perfectionism is negative as it makes you fall out of favour with others, as you will have the tendency of looking down on them because they have not attained your standard. At the same time, it may make you unhappy because you would not appreciate yourself and the efforts you have been making on anything because your eyes are fixed on the perfect state.

Habit 12: Commitment

Commitment is not just being Interested, this is the art of doing something you have agreed to do whether it is convenient or not. This habit makes you do what you have agreed to do. This habit makes you not to be impulsive nor rush making decisions knowing fully well that your words are binding you to. They do not just do what they are committed to, but they do it on time. Steve Jobs, the founder of Apple's view on commitment in relation to the success of his organisation is;

> *The quality of a person's life is in direct proportion to their commitment to excellence, regardless of their chosen field of endeavour.*

The design of the Mac wasn't what it looked like, although that was part of it. Primarily, it was how it worked. To design something really well, you have to get it. You have to really know what it's all about. It takes a passionate commitment to really thoroughly understand something, chew it up, and not just quickly swallow it.

My Learning Points (Write down your learning points of this chapter)

....

....

....

Action Points

Habit(s) I want to continue (and when to do so ...
Date)

....

....

....

Habits I want to change (and when to do so ... Date)

....

....

....

Thankfully you have completed the health , relationship and career /business habits chapters.

Pause to reflect on these 3 groups. What do you need to **START, STOP**, do **MORE or do LESS.**

6- Finance Habits

------------୦ଽ------------

Habit 13: 70-30 Money Habit

This is a habit no one teaches you in school . Only those seeking financial literacy or independence develop it. It is never spend more than 70% of your earning and committing the rest to specific pots that grow it. For you to be able to develop this habit you must make budget a tool you live by. This will almost guarantee that you are on the path to financial freedom. The remaining 30 % should be equally shared between investment, savings and charity (Giving to a cause).

It develops a sense of financial roundness or wholeness and fulfilment, knowing that all areas of your life that need financial attention are covered.

Your discipline muscles will be very useful here as you must find yourself not living out of your plan or budget except in unforeseen contingency.

Habit 14: Saving Habit

You don't ever say, "That's not in my budget this month," this implies that you've got an image to uphold. Living to please others or is it that you have no financial plan that you always have extra money available for any impromptu spending. Practise delayed gratification. It's highly rewarding and also helps build your self-discipline and esteem.

It is so refreshing to hear people reply to a social request with something genuine like, "I have other priorities for my money this month." Choose how to spend your money based on your values. When a decision doesn't fit, recognize that - and acknowledge it with a statement that reflects what is important to you.

There is something incredibly satisfying about saving up for things in advance. In our current world of easy credit, this isn't a satisfaction people get to experience enough of. Go ahead and give it a try. You will be amazed at how you will feel.

Habit 15: Borrowing Habit

This is the act of using or getting money with the intention of returning the same amount or plus interest. This act has been made to be so common that you hardly find any household without significant amount of debt.

The concept of 'enjoy now and pay later' which negates the success of delayed gratification is the order of the day. The rate at which people just buy is alarming.

The amount of lending to individuals increase every day, and this has put most household in a situation that financial freedom seems unattainable or never considered.

People hardly give it a serious thought before borrowing money because lending has been packaged in such a way that you get into it without giving it a second thought.

With the general knowledge that you cannot have a good credit rating without having and using a credit card, is the 1st trap that everyone step into without being mentally prepared for how to make it work for you. It's a battle only a few people win.

In trying to build your credit rating, you get into the habit of using the credit card and before you know it debt starts amassing.

Please do not get me wrong, I am not saying that you should not get a credit card, but what I am saying is that you only use it when you are ready and know the full implications of borrowing.

You must have a good understanding of how it works, and your self-control muscles must have been built and toned. If you cannot self-regulate yourself, you will buy what you do not need with borrowed money (credit).

We must always remember that the borrower is always at the whims and caprices of the lender.

There are 2 types of debt/borrowing;

     i.   *The good debt* is one that is a sensible investment in your financial future; this should always leave you better off in the long-term and should not have a negative impact on your overall financial position.

With this, you will have a clear and specific purpose for the borrowing with a realistic plan for paying it back that allows you to clear the debt as quickly as possible. A plan must always be in place at the beginning to liquidate the debt.

The plan includes identifying the cheapest way of borrowing and a practical way of getting money to pay back. Always have the intention of paying back.

Examples of good debt are; Student loan, Mortgage, Investing in your own business, etc.

ii.   *The Bad debt* is the one that drain your wealth, is not affordable and offer no real prospect of 'paying for itself' in the future.

Bad debts are also likely to have no realistic repayment plans and are often run up when people make impulsive purchases of items they don't really need, or borrow money to pay every day bills.

Does that seem like someone you know? The borrowing habit has crippled a lot of people emotionally and they live depressed because of the financial burden on them. We have heard or read of suicide cases resulting from the pressure or burden of huge debt. If this is your state, meet financial advisers to help you out and while working on that, start working on yourself. The topics of Goal setting and Discipline that are also covered in this book would help you not to just get you out of the financial mess, but also set you on a journey that can lead you to financial freedom if you so desire it.

If you can't afford to borrow the money (i.e you aren't sure of making the monthly/instalment repayments without a default), it is definitely a bad debt.

Examples of bad debts are; luxury holiday you can't afford, A brand new car you don't need and borrowing money to pay bills and or other credit commitments.

If you are struggling to get to the end of the month, you can get money or financial confidential advice, which will help you get your finances back on track.

The following are tips for borrowing wisely if you must borrow;

Ask yourself the following questions. If any of the answers is 'no', that debt is likely to go bad.

- Will borrowing this money improve my finances in the long run?
- Have I shopped around to get the best deal?
- Am I borrowing this money as cheaply as possible?
- Will I be able to cope should interest rates rise in the future?
- Will I comfortably be able to afford the monthly repayments?
- Do I understand all the terms and conditions associated with borrowing this money?

> ➢ Do I understand the risks and what could happen if things go wrong?

Another question to ask yourself if you must borrow is;

How much should I borrow?

Once you have established that the money you want to borrow is a good debt, you need to work out exactly how much to borrow and how you are going to pay it back.

Borrowing more than you need without a plan for paying it back can swiftly turn a good debt bad.

Borrowing must be intentional; therefore, you cannot be casual about it.

My Learning Points (Write down your learning points of this chapter)

....
....
....

Action Points

Habit(s) I want to continue (and when to do so ... Date)

....
....
....

Habits I want to change (and when to do so ... Date)

....
....
....

How well do you rate in the Finance habits just read in this chapter? Is there one or more habit you need to START, STOP, do MORE or LESS.

Make an action plan now!

Rise Up and Do It"!

7- Personal/Self Development Habits

------------₢------------

These are habits that have been presented to us as principles of success. They are generic and common denominators to any success equation. This is a habit of giving up your blame list and channelling your energy to what would improve you. It is not what happens that determine your future, but what you do with what happens. Personal development is increasing your value. These are habits formed to become a valuable person. You are paid according to your value. Becoming a person of value is very crucial in the equation of success. This can only be achieved by working harder on yourself than on your job or business. Life is in seasons you cannot change, but you can change yourself to get the best of the seasons.

Read that book, attend that seminar/workshop, get that mentor and get the coach that keeps you on track.

Always be on the journey of continuous self-improvement.

Habit 16: Accepting and Taking Responsibility

For you to live a meaningful progressive life, you must make a habit of taking responsibility for yourself. Don't play the blame-game with your life!

The first human creation played this game and landed him in an unpleasant situation. Blaming your parents, spouse, friends, colleagues, weather, environment employer and the government or society except yourself is dangerous. This in simple terms means that other people or factors you are blaming are the ones with the control over your life. That's not true, and you know that. Why not start and continue to take responsibility for your life?

If you do not have this singular habit, there is none you can ever consciously develop or improve. Most in secured people are very familiar with this and that is why you will find them blame everyone and everything except themselves. Until you take full responsibility for your life, no meaningful change can be seen or made to move you toward your goal(s) in life. When you do not take responsibility, you allow others and circumstances to take control of your life.

Every human being has been created with the mind that has the power to make choices, which is what is referred to as willpower. We are all a reflection of the choices we make. The choices you make will either move you towards or away from your goals in life.

You may be equipped with the knowledge you need to achieve your goal, but if you are not in control of your life vehicle, you will never be able to drive it to the desired destination. Simply put, accepting and taking responsibility for your life means you are resolved not to make excuses and accept that your achievement or failure is as a result of choices you have made.

I have discovered that most people really want or desire the good stuff in life plus all the habits that will take them there. However, they really want to *Do* , *Be* or *Have* those good things, rather than start on the journey, they take a long vacation to a wonderful fantasy place *Brian Tracy* calls "Someday Isle"

This is the place where the general saying is *'Someday I'll read that book. Someday, I'll start that exercise program. Someday, I'll upgrade my skills and earn more money. Someday, I'll get my finances under control and get out of debt. Someday, I'll do all those things that I know I need to do to achieve all my Goals. Someday.*

Probably 80 percent of the population live on Someday Isle most of the time. They think and dream and fantasize about all the things they are going to do "someday." And who are they surrounded by on Someday Isle? Other people on Someday Isle! And what is the chief topic of conversation on Someday Isle? Excuses! They all sit around and swap excuses for being on the island'.

"Why are you here?" they ask each other. Not surprising, their excuses are largely the same: *"I didn't have a happy childhood, " "I didn't get a good education, " "I don't have any money, " "My boss is really critical, " "My marriage is not good, " "No one appreciates me, "* or *"The economy is terrible. "They now all come down with the disease of* "excusitis," which is invariably fatal to success or achieving any worthy goal. They all have good intentions, but as everyone knows, "The road to hell is paved with good intentions.

"Excusitis" is the inflammation of excuses; as you know in medical science, the inflammation of any organ is usually named to end with "tis". For example, inflammation of the pancreas is pancreatitis!

> *An average person with average talent and education can outstrip the most brilliant genius in our society. If that person has a clear set goals.*
> Brian Tracy

Seriously! How long are you going to continue to live on this island? Get Out of that place and Get on Board with your purpose and start doing what you need to do to your desired destination in life. Vote yourself out of the Island.

Without this habit of accepting or taking responsibility for your life, you cannot set goals and achieve them. You will find yourself living other people's plans, desires, goals and dreams. Be courageous and make that decision now, if you are yet to take full responsibility for your life. *Rise Up and Do It!*

Habit 17: Goal Setting

A goal is defined as: the aim or object towards which an endeavour is directed and the terminal point of a journey or race. Simply put it's a plan with a date.

Life is a journey, and there are several milestones on this journey. To get to the end and cover all the milestones require us becoming a character that takes you through the path. Becoming that character, would involve developing empowering habits to that you through.

Can you imagine setting out from your home to go somewhere at a particular time without planning the time to set out, the mode of transportation to use, route and not knowing the cost of getting there. Do you know that is exactly how most people run their lives?

When you set goals you have clear aims and objectives, and this determines what and how you channel your energy and other resources. Your goals are positive(I hope) statements of intent, well-formed, made with absolute commitment and followed through with daily action.

Successful people are goal oriented. They take their time to identify what they want and build a clear, detailed picture of how to achieve it. They also create a picture of how it will feel like achieving the goal.

Setting goals give purpose, direction and motivation to your life. Do you spend more time planning your holiday than you do your life? Do you spend more planning your wedding than your marriage?

The 7 Habits of effective People by Stephen Cove says; *"To begin with the end in mind means to start with a clear understanding of your destination. It means to know where you are going so that you better understand where you are now and so that the steps you take are always in the right direction. "*

If you do not have a plan or goal, you will live other people's plan. Without goals you drift, and loose control. If you're not in control someone else is. That means you have relinquished your right to shape your own destiny. In doing so, you have surrendered your freedom of action which restricts your choices. This leads to frustration, anxiety, fear and stress.

Your Focus Becomes Your Reality

You get what you focus on. The subconscious mind will work to achieve what you think about most of the time, whether you want them or not *(hence my taking time to explain in the first chapter the link between your thoughts and habits).*

Here is a game that you can play over the next few week with one or two friends.

Set yourself some observation goals. For example, notice the blue cars on your journey home on a particular day, notice the number of sales on TV, in the newspapers or in the shops; or notice the people wearing aftershave or perfume. Choose any potential subject. One key issue here is to note the effect that setting goals have upon your perception.

Ask a person who has been noticing blue cars, how many red cars there were on the road?

What does this Exercise teach you?

If you are the type that has the habit of setting goals , you will find the process of the exercise beneficial for reviewing your own goals.

Stages in Goal setting

There are 10 stages to setting goals, but since this book is not mainly about goals, I will just touch on the first five steps.

1. **Gather:** Put on paper *who you want to be, all you want to do and have in life*. I mean write down everything. It gives you the big picture of your destination. (This exercise alone can take time. please do it)

2. **Review**: Trim down your list to the most important things especially those aligning with your values. Ask what makes it important.

Review your list viz a viz the following; Family, Friends, Spouse/Partner, career/business, financial, health/wellness, social life, fun and recreation, home/environment, spirituality/faith, work/life balance, Task/time management, retirement, contribution to the society/Charity and personal development/growth.

At this point, you may want to go over your list , add, change and delete items on your list in the order of their importance to you. Rank your list in the order of its impact in your life.

3. **Evaluate**: measure your goals against your criteria of values

4. **Action**: What are you willing to do? When will you do it?

5. **Time**: Set specific dates for the action

Any goal set should have a basic feature of S. M. A. R. T i. e. *S*pecific, *M*easurable, *A*chievable, *R*elevant and *T*ime-bound.

A goal is a dream with a date.

Habit 18: Self-Discipline

Discipline is the bridge between setting goals and accomplishing them. Discipline, simply put, is doing what you should do whether you feel like or not, when you should do it. It is doing what you need to do regardless of your feelings. Self-discipline can also be defined as self-control. Your ability to control yourself and make your thoughts, and actions align with your set goals .

Discipline could be expressed in self-denial or delayed gratification. This requires that you deny yourself the easy pleasures. Make yourself do only those things that you know are right for the long-term and appropriate for the moment. Delayed gratification is a form of self discipline. It is the ability to put off satisfaction in the short term in order to enjoy greater rewards in the long run.

None of the habits in this book can be developed or improved without discipline and self-control. We often hear people say "I am not that disciplined", or "I'm not a disciplined person". Discipline never comes by wishful thinking, it has o be intentional.

Discipline Shows Up

If you have imbibed this habit, it shows up in all areas of your life. Let me share with you an example of a work colleague of mine named Alex. You just can't help but notice one who has this empowering habit. In her words she says, "I wonder how people think they can have a good and orderly life without discipline". One day, she indulged herself in an extra bar of chocolate only for me to hear her say to herself that she must do an extra 20 minutes' walk to negate the effect of the additional calories she has taken. What! I was amazed at her utterance; yeah you may be saying oh that is extreme, it's a shame that is the problem we all face and refuse to check the cause of not getting our desired results in life. How can you keep doing the same thing and expect a different result in life!

Alex obviously has her focus on her health goal(s), and I was not surprised when I knew the decision was made few years before the time to change her lifestyle to suit how she really wants it to be.

Why do you think she does what she does? To prove a point? Of course not! Her focus is on her living a healthy and she is committed to whatever it takes to make is happen. Her focus is not allowing herself to slip off the path of her goals. Hence, she disciplines her body and mind to align with it. She understands the law of cause and effect; for every action or inaction there is resultant effect(outcome). So she had to enjoy the effect of her decision to take that extra chocolate bar whether it is convenient or not. If she does not enjoy her extra walk of course, that will influence her decision when next she is faced with a temptation of a bar of chocolate.

No more excuses! "Rise *Up and Do It*". Stop using your incredible brain to think up, elaborate rationalizations and justifications for not taking action.

It has been said that if people put as much energy into achieving their goals as they spend making up excuses for failure, they would actually surprise themselves. But first, you have to vote yourself off the island.

Go develop your Discipline Muscles, you need it! I discovered that you can achieve almost any goal you set for yourself if you have the discipline to pay (or enjoy) the price, to do what you need to do, and to never give up. Without Self-discipline, no principle or habit will ever work.

Make yourself do what you have to do if you are really serious about it. Do something. Do anything. Get on with it! Repeat to your-self: "If it's to be, it's up to me!"

Habit 19: Excellence

Mediocrity seems to be the reigning order of the day. It is very easy to be mediocre. All you have to do is make no extra effort of any kind and drift through life making no difference in the world. You probably won't even be noticed or stand out because there are millions of other people who are also mediocres. But if you will dare to form the habit of being excellent in all that you do, you will be a bright light in the dark world.

Excellence is doing the best you can in every situation, but it is not necessarily perfection. Perfection puts you in bondage of *displeasure* and *frustration*. Excellence is extremely high quality and a virtue to be pursued. Edwin Bliss said, *"The pursuit of excellence is gratifying and healthy. The pursuit of perfection is frustrating, neurotic, and a terrible waste of time. "*

It is worthy to note the difference between striving for excellence and striving for perfection. If you don't, you would end up being frustrated and feel like a failure every step of the way. Did you know that some of the people who procrastinate have perfectionist's traits? They feel compelled to do a perfect job and fear that they won't be able to achieve it, so they put off the task. We tend to think that procrastinators are lazy, and maybe some are. But most are not lazy, they are fearful of falling below others' expectations. It is actually a wonderful thing to realize that as human beings with flaws and weaknesses, we rarely do all things perfectly.

An excellent habit repeated over time will give you the attitude and the result is unimaginable and gratifying.

There was a time in the society when excellence was fairly normal, but that is not the case today. Our passion for more, which is greed, has driven us to prefer quantity instead of quality, and that is sad. Stephen R. Covey said, "*Doing more things faster is no substitute for doing the right things.*"

Make a commitment to habitually pursue excellence and following through this commitment is very rewarding. There is nothing about mediocrity that makes us feel good inside about ourselves or our choices. Rather it makes you look like a commoner doing what everyone does.

If you want to form a habit of being excellent, develop some kind of system to help you remember to press past the point of comfort. It is easy to vacuum clean in the middle of the room, but to do an excellent job, you may have to get under the furniture and move a few things out of the way.

Pressing into excellence won't be easy at first, but eventually it will become a habit and you won't be comfortable unless you do everything you do in the best way possible. You can become a big fan of signs or notes to help you remember while we are forming new habits. Make five signs that simply say EXCELLENCE and place them strategically where you will see them several times a day. *"Rise Up and Do It"*

Habit 20: Giving Back Habit

This is a habit that stems from the act of kindness. It considers and nurtures the need of others (people or community). It is making conscious effort to meet the need without expecting reward from the beneficiaries.

Besides feeling good about yourself for doing something for others, giving back is also good for your physical health. In Canada, studies show that 85% of volunteers rated their health as "good," compared to 79% of non-volunteers. Only 2% of volunteers reported "poor" health, one-third the amount of non-volunteers who reported the same health status.

The studies also show a relationship between volunteering and increased self-esteem. The volunteers recorded both greater personal empowerment and better health. The act of helping others stimulates the release of endorphins, which has been linked to an improved nervous and immune system functions.

Volunteering has been found to help fight depression. Helping others can help take your mind off your own problems and enable you to see the bigger picture. Once you see the difference you can make in another person's life, your own problems seem smaller and more manageable.

Further studies show that people with fewer social contacts have shorter life spans than people with wide social circles, regardless of race, income level or other lifestyle factors. If you are lonely or live in an area far away from friends and family, volunteering is one way to build a social life and improve your emotional and physical health at the same time.

Your act of giving back could be in a regular donation to a good cause or act of service. For instance as a professional, you may give certain level of pro bono services yearly for those who need it but cannot afford. Just Rise Up and Do It!

Identify what is dear to your heart, it could be a good cause to promote or bad one tor stop and launch your plan of action to do something. Write your legacy with what you do for your community and country.

Check out the following 7 more reasons to develop or improve on the habit of giving back (volunteering);

1. *Developing new skills*. Gaining skills, knowledge and expertise are given benefits of volunteering. Giving others your time brings you interesting and challenging opportunities

that might not come along otherwise. This experience can be added to your resume and could result in a better paying job.

I identify with this very reason. It clearly helped me when I relocated to the UK. Though I did not plan to seek paid employment immediately because I was pregnant, but I found it boring not to be active doing something. However I told myself that there must be something I can do before I have my baby.

I offered my time to a church of England church I was attending, letting them know I was happy to help with the church finances if help is needed. Unknown to me that the Priest was a Chief Executive of a big charity organisation . I ended up volunteering in the Finance Department of that organisation. I worked there until I had my baby. What did this volunteering do for me?

- The opportunity to understand the work ethics of the organisation which is a mirror of the society

- Met and interacted with people that helped me with information about the charity sector, accounting profession and the country which was needed helpful .

- I had the volunteering role on my CV which I know opened doors for me later on when I went into paid employment

- Gave me a gratifying feeling that I am needed knowing that I was contributing indirectly to the beneficiaries of the charity.

1. *Making social connections*. Loneliness and boredom are common among retirees, students, and transplants to a new city. Volunteering can relieve this sense of social isolation and help you fill empty hours in the day.

2. *Give back to your community.* Doing something for the community you live in or have lived in. Returning the favour to those who have helped you are strong motivators. Everyone, rich or poor, take from the society, and volunteering is one way to show a sense of

appreciation. There is an adage that says *'A tree does not make a forest'.* This implies that no matter how well endowed you are intellectually or in riches, you still need someone. Giving back is a way to fill the vacuum in others and yours as well.

3. *Develop and grow as a person*. Volunteering is an excellent way to explore your likes and dislikes. If you're interested in a new career, volunteer in the field first to see if you will actually like it. You may find that a totally unrelated field is a much better fit for you, one you'd never consider if you hadn't volunteered there first.

4. *A new perspective.* Life can be challenging, and when you're feeling down, your problems can seem insurmountable. The act of giving back can offer a new perspective—seeing people who are worse off than you are, yet still hanging in there, can help you see your life in a completely different way from how you are seeing it.

5. *You are a resource needed.* Feeling needed and appreciated are important, and you may not get that appreciation from your paid work or home life where the things you do could be easily taken for granted before it is an expectation met. When you volunteer, you realize just how much you are truly needed. Meeting people who need your help is a strong incentive to continue—people depend on you. If you don't do it, who will? There is a problem you are created to solve. These problems are wrapped in the needs of the people around you. Rise up and Do S solve the problem.

6. *Boost your self-esteem.* Most volunteers experience a sense of increased self-esteem and greater self-worth. Helping others make you feel good about yourself because you're doing something for someone that they couldn't do for themselves.

Research has shown that the good feelings you experience when helping others may be just as important to your health as exercise and a healthy diet. But it's the smile from a child or thankful person that shows you're really making a difference in someone's life. And that's the greatest feeling in the world.

Whatever you give back, the universe has a way of responding to you by meeting your own needs too.

What are you giving?

Bill Gates, Warren Buffet and Oprah Winfrey, to mention a few, though all wealthy are intentional about giving back to the universe. Don't you think there is something in this. Take an audit on your potentials and resources, then Rise Up and Do something. Let the world stage know you are here by you playing your part on the stage too.

"Rise Up and Do It"

My Learning Points
(Write down your learning points of this chapter)

....

....

....

Action Points

Habit(s) I want to continue (and when to do so ... Date)

....

....

....

Habits I want to change (and when to do so ... Date)

....

....

....

How well do you rate in the Finance habits just read in this chapter? Is there one or more habit you need to START, STOP, do MORE or LESS.

Make an action plan now!

Rise Up and Do It"!

8 - Get Started Now!

------------∞------------

"A journey of a thousand miles begins with one step." Lao-Tzu

T he biggest thief of success is procrastination. We can think about doing the right thing, plan to do it, and talk about doing it, but nothing changes in our lives until we start consistently doing what we need to do. Perhaps, you have so many bad habits that you feel overwhelmed, and you are not even sure that you can develop the habits highlighted in this book, you are not alone. Read on and you will discover HOW to do this.

You would like to change, but you're not sure if you want to change. "BAD HABITS ARE LIKE A COMFORTABLE BED, EASY TO GET INTO, BUT HARD TO GET OUT OF."

Bruce Barton said, *"What a curious phenomenon it is that you can get men to die for the liberty of the world that will not make the little sacrifice that is needed to free themselves from their own individual bondage."*

Are you willing to make sacrifice and do the more difficult things now in order to enjoy a life of freedom later on? The irony is that we are often unwilling to suffer for a short while, then we end up with continual misery, dread, guilt, and the penalties of having put off something that would have taken a few minutes or a few hours to do. In other words, by putting off the "pain" of doing something hard, we often spend much more time avoiding it than it would take to just do it.

We all have good and bad habits, but Benjamin Franklin said, *"Your net worth to the world is usually determined by what remains after your bad habits are subtracted from your good ones."* Get started right now forming all the good habits you can. Soon, they will outnumber the bad ones, and your value to yourself, your family, your friends and society will increase exponentially.

Defeat Procrastination

"If you have goals and procrastination, you have nothing. If you have goals and you take action, you will have anything you want." Thomas J. Vilord

Procrastination is a thief, and it deceives us. It makes us complacent by telling us that we are going to do the right thing. It justifies inactivity.

A story is told about three demons who were graduating from their course on how to deceive and prevent people from knowing the Truth about themselves i. e. their potentials and abilities. The Head of the demons was questioning each one on how to accomplish this mission. The first one answered that he would tell people there was no Truth. The Head answered, "You won't deceive many because most people deep down inside of them know that they have the potential and abilities even if they have not been courageous enough to explore their possibilities in life"

The second demon said he would tell people that their potentials and abilities play no part in them becoming who they want to be. The Head said' "You will deceive a few more than your co-worker, but not many.

"The third demon said that he would tell people that there was no hurry, and they could put off the decision to maximise their potentials and utilise their abilities until another time. This response got the Head demon excited, and he said, "You will definitely get many people by simply telling them to make the decision later." Procrastination steals your time, your potential, self-esteem and peace of mind. It is like a lullaby that whispers, "Go to sleep; everything will be fine." But everything will not be fine if we put off doing what we need to do. And the task isn't going to get done by itself! It's not going anywhere. Procrastination can only be conquered by becoming what I call a "now" person. Be aggressive when you know you need to do something. Don't keep putting things off ... just do it!

Putting things off aggravate us. We may not even be consciously aware of it, but unfinished projects mount pressure on us. If you walk through your home and see dishes in the sink, laundry on the floor, trash cans filled to the brim, beds unmade, every countertop piled high with mail that needs to be sorted This puts pressure on you in some way. You may even get so irritated or grouchy that you find yourself starting an argument with someone else in the house just because you feel overwhelmed. When we find fault with someone else, it diverts attention from how we feel about ourselves. Procrastination never makes us feel good.

Cultivate or form the habit of being a **"now"** person, one who does what needs to be done as soon as possible regardless of the situation. All truly successful people have this habit. *"Rise Up and Do It"*

"Procrastination is suicide on an instalment plan.

Author Unknown

Action! Action! Action!

"We become just by performing just actions, temperate by performing temperate actions, brave by performing brave actions" **_Aristotle_**

Don't wait to "feel" like doing a thing before you do it. Live by decision, not emotion. Experience has taught me that the more I sit around and do nothing, the more I want to sit around to do nothing, but if I get up and get moving, then energy begins to flow. Activity is like flipping on a light switch. The power is there all the time, but it is not ignited until you flip the switch. We always have the ability to be active, but no energy flows until we actually get moving. Ask those that have made an exercise routine a part-time job, they are always bubbling with energy that can be put into good use if they choose to do so. *Rise Up and Do It* !

It's Time

Make a list of all the habits you want to make and all the ones you want to break. Now, choose one and use the principles in this book to help you. If you focus, one at a time, on the habits you want to make, eventually they'll become second nature. If you focus— one at a time—on those you want to break (by doing the exact opposite of the habit), eventually you will conquer them all. But if you look at them all at once, you will feel overwhelmed and be defeated before you even begin. Working toward a change is much easier if we take one thing, one day at a time, and stick with it until we experience breakthrough. Don't ever be discouraged because you have not arrived at success, instead, be pleased that you are pressing toward it.

Little drops make the mighty ocean. Start small and grow with it. Discouragement will only zap the strength you need to eventually succeed.

Often, the magnitude of challenge stops people from taking action. Facebook did not start as it is ; it went through a metamorphosis before finally becoming what you see today. Mark Zuckerberg used the concept of the site in other formats first. *'Taking action is breathing life into the life of an idea'.*

Achievers put themselves on the hot seats rather than waiting for all conditions to be right. They drive the conditions to suit them rather than otherwise. This develops confidence and boldness in them which is what they use to tackle any new idea they have.

You could be the solution to the problems prevalent around you. If you can be courageous enough to move that idea you have into action now.

30-60-100 Principle

This is a principle derived from an age- long parable that I will share with you;

"Once there was a man who went out to sow grain. As he scattered the seed in the field, some of it fell along the path, and the birds came and ate it up. Some of it fell on rocky ground, where there was little soil. The seeds soon sprouted, because the soil wasn't deep. Then, when the sun came up, it burned the young plants; and because the roots had not grown deep enough, the plants soon dried up. Some of the seeds fell among thorn bushes, which grew up and choked the plants, and they didn't bear grain. But some seeds fell in good soil, and the plants sprouted, grew, and bore grain: some had thirty grains, others sixty, and others one hundred. "

The seed referred to in the story is synonymous to information that you get through any means of which one is reading this book. The different types of soil in the story refer to the state of the mind of the recipient of the information. The "30-60-100 yield" is the result of planting the seed on the different types of good soil. For you to have gotten to this page, you must be good soil as seen in the parable, the seeds that landed in the good soil yielded 30%, 60% and 100% respectively. *Why the varying percentile result?* The outcome is as a result of the proportion of your reception and subsequent action taken in response to the information.

If you have information that has the potential of giving you a 100% and you only get 60% or 30%, then it's not as a result of your level of information received, but the committed action that followed. You will only get the result proportionate to the level of action.

Action

Having brilliant ideas means nothing unless you're prepared to take action.

"Action is the foundational key to all success". Pablo Picasso

By taking action, you breathe life into the idea. The old doctrine of ready, aim and fire is being replaced by fire, fire and fire! You're far better taking off action – adjusting –adjusting taking action-assessing; taking action and adjusting, rather than just planning, planning, planning.

One of the most impressive things I noticed about achievers was their speed when it comes to take action. They call rather than email. They ask for decisions to be made now. They make commitments and go for it. They shrink time scales. They do it fast. They do it now.

My Learning Points (Write down your learning points of this chapter)

....

....

....

Action Points

Habit(s) I want to continue (and when to do so ... Date)

....

....

....

Habits I want to change (and when to do so ... Date)

....

....

....

9- HOW? HOW? HOW?
------------ℭ℞------------

Get Rid of Your Loser's Limp

Loser's limp is a *built in excuse* that makes you think you have a genuine reason for not been able to get a task done. It can stop you from creating a new habit or stopping an old habit that does not support your goals in life.

Excuses are what make you use your background, age, race colour or sex as a reason for not doing what you have the ability to do.

Do you know that what you focus on becomes your reality? Take responsibility for your thoughts and words and begin choosing them carefully because they are the raw material for your actions and inevitably your destiny.

Let me share the inspiring story of a man named *Cliff Young.*

Cliff Young is hardly known outside of Australia. His remarkable story is worth knowing, though. Australians thought he was a crazy old man to undertake an almost impossible feat. Most feared that he would die trying.

Every year, Australia hosted an 875-kilometre endurance race from Sydney to Melbourne – considered at the time to be the world's longest and toughest ultra-marathon. The few highly-trained world-class athletes that participated averaged around 30 years old, and were mainly sponsored by major brands and thus competed with the latest and finest running gear. The race usually took a week to complete.

In 1983, everyone was in for a surprise. On the day of the race, a guy named Cliff Young showed up. At first, no one cared about him since everybody thought he was there to watch the event. After all, he was 61 years old and was wearing overalls and gumboots.

As Cliff walked up to the table to take his number, it became obvious to everybody he was a participant. He was going to join a group of 150 world-class athletes run! They all thought that it was a crazy publicity stunt. Curiosity was raised as he took his number "64", pinned it to his overalls, and moved into the pack of runners kitted in their special, expensive racing outfits. The camera focused on him, and reporters started to ask:

"Who are you and what are you doing?"

"I'm Cliff Young. I'm from a large ranch where we run sheep outside of Melbourne. "

"Are you really going to run in this race?"

"Yeah," Cliff nodded.

"Got any backers?"

"No. "

"Then you can't run."

"Yeah I can," Cliff said. "See, I grew up on a farm where we couldn't afford horses or four-wheel drives, and the whole time I was growing up – until about four years ago when we finally made some money and got a four wheeler – whenever the storms would roll in, I'd have to go out and round up the sheep. We had 2000 head, and we have 2000 acres. Sometimes I would have to run those sheep for two or three days. It took a long time, but

I'd catch them. I believe I can run this race; it's only two more days. Five days. I've run sheep for three. "

When the marathon started, the pros left Cliff behind. The crowds smiled because he set off in his gumboots, and his technique was "incorrect". Instead of running, he traipsed along with a leisurely shuffle.

All over Australia, people who watched the live telecast kept on praying that someone would stop this crazy 61-year-old farmer, concerned that he would die before getting even halfway across Sydney.

Every professional athlete knew for certain that it took about 7 days to finish this race and that in order to compete; you would need to run 18 hours and sleep 6 hours. The thing is 61 year old Cliff Young did not know that!

When the morning news of the race was aired, people were in for another big surprise. Cliff was still in the race and rather than stopping to sleep had jogged all night down to a city called Mittagong.

When asked about his race tactics, he said it was "to run to the finish line."

And so he kept running. Every night he got just a little bit closer to the leading pack. By the last night, he passed all of the world-class athletes, while they were sleeping. He remained ahead until the finish line. Not only did he run the Melbourne to Sydney race at age 61, without dying; he won first place, breaking the race record by 9 hours!

Sixty-one-year-old Cliff Young finished the 875-kilometre race in 5 days, 15 hours and 4 minutes. He didn't sleep because he didn't know that he was supposed to; he just kept imagining that he was chasing sheep and trying to outrun a storm.

When Cliff was awarded the first prize of $10 000, he said he did not know there was a prize and insisted that he had not entered for the money. He said, "There are 5 other runners still out there doing it tougher than me," and he gave them $2 000 each.

In the following year, Cliff Young entered the same race and achieved 7th place. While running, his hip popped out of the joint socket, his knee played up, and he endured shin splints. But that didn't deter him from finishing the race. When he was announced as the winner for most courageous runner and presented with a

Mitsubishi Colt, he said, "I didn't do it near as tough as old Bob McIlwaine. Here, Bob, you have the car," and gave the keys to him.

Cliff never kept his race winnings or any of the numerous gifts he received, he rather gave it away to someone who seemed to need it more.

Cliff came to prominence again in 1997, at age 76 when he attempted to become the oldest man to run around Australia and raise money for homeless children. He managed to complete 6,520km of the 16000km run before he had to pull out after his only permanent crew member became ill.

In Cliff's last race, he completed the full 921 km, not bad, considering that he was 78 years old!

It's fascinating how often unremarkable people feature in the most remarkable stories. It's also inspiring because there's probably a Cliff Young in every one of us so Rise *Up and Do It!*

What Decision are you willing to make now?

Reprogramming and Repetition

Reprogram Yourself

It's amazing how powerful your subconscious mind is. Every single time you do something, your subconscious programs it into your brain. The more you do it, the more entrenched the program becomes. I have been amazed at how difficult it is for me to start a new task and how much easier it gets each time I do it again and again.

Each time you start a new task challenge, your subconscious remembers it, and it is easier the next time. Human beings are created in an amazing way that has enabled you to become an excellent person, simply through doing the best things over and over again until you become excellent at it.

Charles Dickens said, "I could never have done what I have done without the habits of punctuality, order, and diligence, without the determination to concentrate myself on one subject at a time."

Though he has the *t*remendous gift of storytelling, but he still had to form good habits of concentration, order, and diligence to be a good steward of his talent. Many people are talented but don't bother to form good habits. They won't discipline themselves to do what they know they should do, but instead they wait to be moved by some outside force.

Repetition

Repetition is the key to forming habits, good or bad. When working toward forming a good habit, you may have to leave notes for yourself as reminders to do the good thing you are aiming for.

The bad habits in our lives hinder us from being the people we want to be. When an enemy is trying to destroy you, you cannot show it mercy.

Deal with bad habits relentlessly. Find ways to help yourself do the good things that you truly want to do. Don't fail to realize that bad habits steal your worthy goals in life.

Don't for a second think, "Oh, it's just a bad habit; it's not that big a deal." With such thinking, you will more than likely never conquer that habit. Say to yourself instead, "This bad habit is my enemy. It is stealing the quality of life I want to have and it's moving me away from the life I want, I am not going to permit it to remain in my life".

- John had a bad habit of hitting the snooze button on his alarm too many times, and he was consistently late for work. He had to break this habit as it was becoming clear he was on the verge of losing his job because of this habit, so he moved the alarm clock across the room to force him to get out of bed to turn it off. In doing this, things, he was dealing aggressively not only with his bad habit, but also with the thief that was about to take his job away.

- Jane's husband drank several glasses of whole milk each day. She was concerned about his fat and cholesterol intake, so she gradually added skimmed milk to the whole-milk carton until eventually; her husband was drinking all skimmed milk. He now says that whole milk tastes weird. This shows how we can gradually get accustomed to something that is better for us and not even miss the thing we previously did.

My Learning Points (Write down your learning points of this chapter)

....

....

....

Action Points

Habit(s) I want to continue (and when to do so ... Date)

....

....

....

Habits I want to change (and when to do so ... Date)

....

....

....

10 - Things You Need To Do Differently

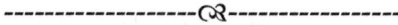

-------------------CR------------------

To change or develop a new habit requires doing things differently. It's just about doing small things differently; making small, consistent changes that give a massive outcome. These Nine tips can be used to improve any area of your life be it; Health, Relationship, Business, Finance or Career.

I. **Be Specific** When you set yourself a target on anything, you need to be as specific as possible. "Lose five pounds" is a better target than "lose some weight," because it gives you a clear idea of what achieving it looks like. Knowing the exact of what you want to achieve keeps you motivated until you get there.

II. **Never Loose any Moment to Act on Your set Target** Given how busy most people are, and how many targets or goals that need to be juggled with at once, it's no surprise that we routinely slip on opportunities to act our goal because we simply fail to notice them. Can you honestly say that you did not have to work out today? Or there was no chance at any point to return that phone call? Achieving your goal means never losing any moment or opportunity before they slip through your fingers.

III. **Know Exactly How Far You Have Left to Go** To achieve any meaningful target in the habit forming or changing process, an honest and regular assessment of the progress—by you and others as appointed by you. If you don't know how well you are doing, you can't adjust your behaviour accordingly. Check your progress frequently—weekly, or even daily, depending on the goal.

IV. **Be a Realistic Optimist** As you set to achieve your goal, it is beneficial to engage in lots of positive thinking because you become your thoughts as you have read in the earlier chapter of this book. Believing in your ability to succeed is enormously helpful in creating and sustaining your motivation. However, in your optimistic state, don't lose sight of the fact that there would be challenges and limitations particularly with timing towards reaching your goal. Most goals worth achieving require time, planning, effort, and persistence. Research shows that just thinking that things will come to you easily and effortlessly leaves you not adequately prepared and significantly increases the odds of failure.

V. **Getting Better over Being Good** Your focus should be on getting better i. e. raising your standard all the time. Many of us believe that our intelligence, our personality, and our physical aptitudes are fixed—that no matter what we do, we won't improve. LIE!! This makes us focus on goals that are all about proving ourselves, rather than developing and acquiring new skills.

VI. **Having Grit is Key.** Grit is a personality trait that shows a willingness to commit to long-term goals and to persist in the face of challenges. Research shows that gritty people obtain more education in their lifetimes. The good news is that if you are not particularly gritty now, there is something you can do about it. People who lack grit, more often than not, believe that they just don't have the innate abilities successful people have. Guess what, you're very wrong. Grit is the expressed ability to persist and commit to a long-term objective or goal.

VII. **Build Your Willpower Muscle** Discipline or self-control "muscle" is just like other muscles in your body; it only gets stronger with frequent and regular exercise (usage). When you give it regular workouts, putting it to good use, it will grow stronger and stronger, and better able to help you successfully reach your goals. Building willpower requires you to take on a challenge to do something you'd honestly rather not do. For instance, giving up high-fat snacks, doing a hundred sit-ups a day or learning a new skill are what many do not think they cannot do but with a well built will power they are achievable. When you find yourself wanting to give in, give up, or just not bothered—don't, that is when to Continue! *"Rise Up and Do It"*

"Discipline is the bridge between goals and accomplishment"

VIII.   **Don't Tempt Fate** No matter how strong your will power is, it's important to always respect the fact that it has its limitation. If you overstretch it, you may snap run out of steam. Don't try to take on two challenging goals at once, if you can help it. This makes achieving your goal easier by sticking to a goal at a time. Sometimes, people can be overly confident in their ability to do many things at a go. Please resist this temptation so that you save yourself from the embarrassment of avoidable failure.

IX.　　　　　Focus

Focus on What You Will Do, Not What You Won't Do

Do you want to get promoted, quit smoking, or put a lid on your bad temper? then plan how you will replace counterproductive behaviours with more constructive and profitable ones. Most of the time, people concentrate all their efforts on what they want to stop doing and fail to consider how they will fill the void. Research on thought suppression has shown that trying to avoid a thought makes it even more active in your mind. The same holds true when it comes to behaviour; by trying not to do something, the impulse gets strengthened. Focus on what you want to do rather than what you do not want to do. *"Rise Up and Do It"*

My Learning Points

(Write down your learning points of this chapter)

....

....

....

Action Points

Habit(s) I want to Continue (And When to do so ... Date)

....

....

....

Habits I want to change (And When to do so by ... Date)

....

....

....

11 – The Challenge

------------∞------------

Decide on which habit(s) you want to Start , Stop ,do More or do Less based on all the four plus one area this book has covered. Set goals on this habit e. g. starting to exercise each day or eating 5 a day portion of the fruit.

Write all the, would - like to start habits (I suggest you pick one at a time) so that you do not overwhelm yourself with too many changes. Every individual has a limit of change they can take per time. Don't stretch your limit to be effective in engraving the habit. Give your-self, time; don't forget it took you a long time of repetition to form what you already have so changing cannot be an overnight activity.

Take Charge

What is the point of sharing the story of Cliff Young? You may have asked yourself while reading this book that it is impossible to change some habits.

Remember!

Cliff Young had no barrier in his mind hence he achieved his set target. Is it not time to bring down all the walls your experience, environment and relationship have erected in your mind that are limiting you to taking appropriate steps to leap into the realm of possibilities. What are you waiting for? What is stopping you? *"Rise Up and Do It"*

Take Charge of your life and take back full control by putting a stop to old disempowering habits and replace them with new ones.

Concentrating on the good habit helps eliminate the bad that is already formed. Trying to stop a bad habit without having a replacement has made a lot of people perpetually enslaved to the habit. Pay more attention to new habit forming or improving rather than paying attention to the one you are trying to stop. Try it and see how it works.

Focus on the benefits, this gives you the energy to do more of the good habit(s) or stop any bad one you have identified.

90-120-180 days challenge

Take the challenge for 90, 120 or 180 days until the new habit becomes part of you. Make yourself accountable to someone that can help you to push forward. Someone who believes in your ability and would not hesitate to let you know when you are deviating or not measuring up to your expectation. Why do you think people hire personal trainers? It is to have someone that paid to hold them accountable and committed to the health goal they have.

If you are still struggling with the changes, then it is advisable that you hire the services of a life coach. A coach is a catalyst that helps YOU get to where you want faster.

A life coach will help you explore the areas of your weakness and identify possible hindering factors that may not be very glaring to you. The coach can help design ways of overcoming those obstacles.

My Learning Points

(Write down your learning points of this chapter)

....

....

....

Action Points

Habit(s) I want to Continue (And When to do so ... Date)

....

....

....

Habits I want to change (And When to do so ... Date)

....

....

....

....

Signing Off

It is not what you know that liberate you or empowers you to live the life you desire, but what you do. '***Rise Up and Do It'*** and watch the universe respond to you. Live the life you desire by designing it with your actions .

Thanks for finishing this book. I would like to know what you think about this book. Please share your thoughts with me by sending a feedback to me on arolanrewaju@gmail.com with the ***Title: Feedback 'Rise up and Do It'***. Please recommend it to someone too if you find it beneficial and of value..

'Rise Up and Do It'   *Atinuke Olanrewaju*

---

i Brian Tracy- miracle of Self Discipline

Stephen R. Covey

www.ingramcontent.com/pod-product-compliance
Lightning Source LLC
Chambersburg PA
CBHW060508030426
42337CB00015B/1795